BPH

BLUEBOY PUBLISHING HOUSE

www.blueboypublishinghouse.com

Published May 22, 2022
ISBN: 979-8-9875302-6-9
Copyright © 2022 Dorian Blue
All rights reserved.

black and blue

Dedication

Interlude: for the sea

The Love Letter

Part I: Black

Part II: Blue

for Gabby

Interlude:
FOR THE SEA

The Love Letter

If I touch you there,
everything about me will be true
A New World discovered
without pick, or axe...

My hand stops midair.

This is a love letter to *the Sea*:
You were all the parts of me
that I was afraid to keep
when your lips touch mine
I feel the waves of the ocean
running to kiss my feet
but Sea, meeting you at the shore
was no easy feat—
I was afraid to be pulled under,
consumed by infinite possibility
when I was in your arms I felt *almost* free
of the baggage tied to my feet
sad to say that I couldn't swim
your depths unfamiliar to me,
I pulled back from your embrace
feeling the waters of desire rise in my chest—
I was afraid to drown.

I write this for the ancestors that tossed
themselves over the sides of slave ships
and into the waters:

see those ancestors became myth,
water-bound sirens who tempt presuming
colonizers who believed, *to their fault*,
that the world was theirs.
despite generations of subjection,
our bodies were never theirs.

these words are written for every
Black body that refuses to be colonized:
we rebel against the norm
we snatch back our mother tongue,
with sharp-witted comebacks that speak
to our agility to flow seamlessly through social scripts
and splash back against routine injustices

we are infinite.
we are free.
we are *unforgivably*, *endlessly* Black.

this love letter is to all the unforgivable
bits of me that I was once afraid to keep:
I want to see you again.

to all the parts of you that you worried were *too extravagant,*
too overbearing,
too much—
you are wrong.
I want them.

I am ready to surf your tides
because by loving *the Sea* I learned to love
all the parts of me that I was afraid to be

See, for *you* I would dive to the depths of the ocean
just to meet you on the ground floor
and love you where you are

you inspire me to perform relentless joy until it becomes second nature —
I love you.

I will continue to dive deep into your waves
I will tread the shore to meet you where you are
I will carry you when the days are low
I will be gentle with you, like a bouquet of
hand-picked flowers from the garden
and I will tend to you,
knowing that you grow like a rose bush
and the thorns come first
but the flowers, *my god are they beautiful*

this poem is for the ancestors that found
their freedom in deep waters
this poem is for the histories we write
with our unforgettable brown skin
and this poem is for *you*.
Because *we* are love
and, through loving *myself*, I learned
that I am love

thank you.

Part I:
BLACK

Testing Grounds

You say that I am divine.

But I am not God(?)

I was told that God was white.

Vengeful, omnipotent, terrible.

He demands sacrifice, blood, age-old tradition.

My skin rebels against the rules.

I crave power, but I will not hold it.

White supremacy is power.

There is pain in power.

Pain will separate me.

Your eyes hold secrecy, depth, magnetism.

I fight the hurricane of my desire.

Love demands sacrifice.

Whose love? Who is to sacrifice?

At last, we have come to the land of the body.

Whose body? Am I the sacrifice?

I was taught to love in sacrifice.

Do you know how to give and receive?

In equal exchange?

My daily dance is a transaction between the dawn and the dark.

A shadow is the   *antithesis*   of what we boast
After the sun is risen   we turn away the night
Nightmares blend into the fading corners of the bedroom
Light reflected   on honey-brown melanin
I was taught to hate my own skin   I buck against *the tradition*
Of bleaching creams   &   skin-brightening treatments
I carry light in my hands   my skin shines without apology

Do you know the shape of *your* shadow?
The darkness conceals things more   *terrible*   than blackness
Sickness takes no days off

Thoughts shatter intent as quickly as you came   running
Unforgivable   excess
Luminous ebony skin

I am consumed by my desire
I am afraid of what consumes me

My shadow is not I.

Blossomin' Bois: An Ode to the Sunflower
by Bridget Jones and Dorian Blue

I wear my hats and briefs fitted,
shoes and crown rope twisted and tied
My bow ties and durags silky.
& My chicken better be fried.
Energy tall. Energy long wit my yellow petal bantu fro
These other seed bearing dreads can't see me.
I be stuntin' in the way I glow.

Sunflowers sprout from our melanated crowns
Delicate. Magical. Insistent.
Soft masculinity represented in shades of brown
We are the buds that bloom with intent.

And we bloom through cement.
We cast our soiled black bodies. We bloom and repent.
No more hiding in darkness.
To the sun we race.
To the ground. To the grime. Attention! About face.

Picked petals pressed between pages
Of our black boi persistence,
We reject a null existence.

No longer will we hide our kaleidoscopic colors,
We rise up, we protect our brothers.
Our black bodies inform resistance.

And we resist definition.
Boihood rough around the edges.
We defy clean-cut boxes.
Our browns bleed and bloom resistance.
Sunflowers rebel and sprout through concrete.
We love our blacks without division.

Are we allowed to be beautiful anyway?
Unalike, yet color coded kindred,
we invoke our gods to defend this,
Lest our light not be apprehended.
Lay siege and witness.
Gender black like all colors blended.
Mold broken.
Edges.... rescinded.

To the sun god which art in heaven
Who gave meaning to thou name
Our kingdom come. Our will be done.
How light differs without the shame?
We blossom bright in indigo fields.
No longer masticating in our flesh.
Our wounds are closing. Colors, unfolding.
With our mouths closed, our petals confess.

Baggage

I make love to you with my bags packed,
nostalgia weighing down my limbs
as your fingers trace me backwards
to the night we first latched eyes,
your caresses tease along my spine
tracing foreign love languages into my skin

Memory is a hand over my willing mouth,
pushing back "I love you" when you test my limits
my body is heavy with old reminders
loss, grief, and *mourning* intertwined
at the same time that my legs wrap
around your steady hips

Your lips brush against my collarbone as
my fears *swallow me*
                  and *swallow me*
                            and *swallow me*
a threesome between *you, me,* and my *pervasive doubt*
I feel intuition, weighty like stones in my gut
heavy like my *baggage*: my spine bows under pressure
of past sins that I will not forget–

I make love to you with my bags packed.

Reckless

And here I am caught, once again–
Straddling a fine line separating worlds of trouble
Breaking the rules that I myself defined

Some things never change,
And it seems I indeed stayed the same:
Living my life in a coward's pause
(That uncertain gap between trying too little,
and wanting too much)

I Won't Sing Along to Complacency

The days of late have gone like a dream
Stumbling around in a hazy stupor and
Falling straight down the rabbit hole
The bitterness I've collected
is a hard pill to swallow;
I refuse to sing along to complacency

I fell asleep to the lull of the impossible,
Not long after waking up to a daze
Is there anything more than this exhausted monotony?
The tired ticking of a weathered clock
Hung on the walls of long work days
The paced tapping on the ground of impatient feet
Matched to more impatient faces,
Exasperated workers pushing one another aside,
Though all in stride to the same tight schedule

The American dream is a rambling speech
Pushing better learning and forced education,
Modified foods marketed as world-hunger-saving
Though never even seen by the mouths of the third world
When does progress stop being a list,
Typed in Times New Roman in font point-12
On clean printer paper and detailing all the goals
We've so far reached since 1776?

When do I start being seen as more than
A taxpayer, or
A student, or
A minority, or
A woman, or
A lifelong debtor, or
A homeless person with no contribution?

Every life no more than a cog in a machine
Yet when was the system last oiled
With kindness and extended consideration for those
That earn less yearly income than the top two percent?

Don't offend me with star-eyed wonder
When quoting a nation built on "liberty"
A network of communities shaming consumers while
Constructing houses on the backs of brittle skeletons
Wake me up from this dream on the day
That I can purchase that "American dream"
Without first selling my soul
When I'm to be considered for more
Than just what I can contribute to my society,
Or what my GPA looks like to you
When placed on a four-point weighted scale;
But instead, weigh for the value of my humanity
We are worth so much more than a handful of statistics.

Mother Womb

we are interconnected

                native and primal

defiant to domestication.

             resistant to explanation.

motherhood is:
        generational pain
        shared experience
        shared bloodline
        shared trauma: in birth, and in delirium

a sealed connection between two souls
our covenant,   *native* and *primal*
a wailing passed back

        from womb to skin,

from marrow to blood.

open conversation,
passed between kindred spirits:

"This is my child."

                    "This is my mother."

native   and   *primal*

                  Won't you be my mother?

Illiterate Tongues

My mouth betrays me,
Words that stick like glue
Or spill like water from my lips
My heathen words discontent
Like many untaught sinners
That rise to judge and spit

My ears crave age old language
Foreign discourse from the Mother Land
My feet rise and resist the carrying on
Hardened soles muddy with dissent
The ground swallows our sorrows

Rebellion is formed by the mother tongue
I have forgotten the harsh dialect of founding fathers
Liberty void upon my lips
I crave the sweetness of still silence
Hollow space formed by illiterate tongues

Our vernacular is shattered
Gaping mouths that scrabble and scratch for meaning
They call us to *rise*, *rebel*, and *decolonize*
Our mother tongue

Toppling

It was a fragile tower,
An unstable Jenga masterpiece made of tentative hope
and the notion that the monsters would sleep
if I only step a bit lighter...
Tiptoe, tiptoe–
Uh-oh.

A little like coming to the edge of a
precipice and looking *down*,
Down...
An unreachable abyss between *you* and *I*
Pain tucked away like secrets in a ravine of the mind,
Prayers tossed up like coins into a wishing well.

She was an enigma to behold,
A sweet-faced treasure with *honeyed words*
A pleasant façade hiding the mortality
                              of fanged bites
Tragedy always left me a bitter taste,
Subtle poisoning masked by dulling waves of shock

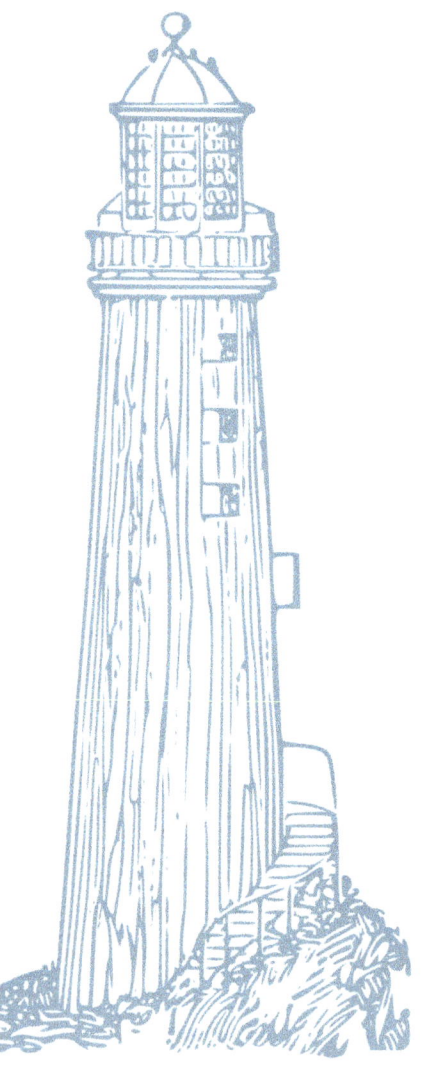

We cut all our losses and took the leap,
Only to miss our mark and land in free-fall
To give up my *crippling fear* of gravity
Only to become a night-time horror,
The feared monster lurking at the bottom of the lake

The screaming was a *terrible* sound–
Like shattered windows masked with a high-pitched siren
It was only a gust of wind that demolished my world;
Balmy enough, but it possessed *a cruel force*.

Losing the Bigot's Game

"All my life I've had to fight,"

> *Except*, as a colored woman,
> I was never let into the ring.

They throw one-two punches
in my direction *and yet*,

> I've been confined to the sidelines indefinitely.

Advance,   ***push***,   fall back;   **no**, press on...
A tireless game of *give* and *take*
Where I **give** all I've got

and

take whatever good comes my way

There are few privileges to being Black

in a bigot's society.

———◇———

"If you can't beat 'em, join 'em."

Except I cannot join them, much less get recognized.

In a society invested with

identity *roles*   and   identity *rules*

Since when does Black have to mean

full of rage, or *uncouth*?

I shouldn't be called a nigger   simply because of my skin tone

It should not be only one or the other,

Either an Oreo   or a stereotype,

Either delinquent   or statistical outlier.

Bigotry does not have authority over my identity.

"You cannot solve a problem with the same mind that created it."

Two hundred years later and things haven't much changed

A different mind and different eyes,

And I was still never able to beat the game

It's skin tone status that bars me from succeeding with grace

But the nuances of my race

        can't be seen on my face.

I said, the nuances of my race

        can't be seen on my face.

The nuances of my identity

        can't be judged by my face.

Interlude:
UNCUT YOUR TONGUE

Why do you hold your tongue?

Perhaps you were taught your words were too weighty for the world to hold — and so you rebel and rage in silence. Or perhaps you fight back words that are sharp enough to wound — and so, as a pacifist, you push back your vitriol.

Your words struggle against the limits you have placed on your tongue. Where have you compromised the unique power of your voice?

Have you grown bitter yet from all the truths unspoken?
Do they roughen your internal world and fracture your worldview?
Where do you safely unpack your overwhelmed emotion,
                     your trembling anger,   and your unmet desire?

Decolonize your silence. Absolve your need to hide behind half-truths and pleasant lies. *Uncut your tongue* — and with that, liberate your truth.

First, I invite you to start with your tongue. Understand the narratives twisted around your roots. Exercise your right to tell your story. And once you have successfully done that work, *I challenge you to speak your mind.*

Part II:
BLUE

This Is The Last Poem I Write For You

The words came out *hot* and *sharp*,
a searing coal on the brain–
COWARD–
burned in my throat like
a large swig of cheap liquor
and forced itself out;
as damning in its nature as
a transgression at a confessional

Loving you was my religion,
and I've lost my faith.
One thousand, five hundred and sixty-two
days in anticipation
A cheapskate disguised as a keepsake,
for grief's sake–
You shut me out of heaven after showing me the light;
I was *almost* saved.
But this is long past *resurrection*,
Emergency-mandated resuscitation,
You rejected my confession–
It was outside of the accepted canon,
And *you* were an atheist.

It was too long and too much for me
to continue to wait,
After four years spent
between idolatry and hate,
Never believing in my heart
that you could come too late.
You broke all my commandments and stayed anyway.
But these sins owe no extra penance:
I paid in full through heartbreak.

You're no Christ figure,
no *savior*,
no *hero*–

That was the last night I saw
the you I knew before
you began to feign
none of it had mattered, after all.
Your heart wasn't in it.

And *you* were not in it–
No, not *you*, not the one with enough faults to break us both
but instead,
A broken young man in the place of Zeus

An idealized deal between my brain and my heart,
that so long absolved to resolve
this arhythmic and discordant melody,
a struggle between reality and blatant self-deception

And this *anger*–
It was the antithesis of leaving my heart wide open
A safe word with more comfort to me
than the feel of your hands at 1 a.m.
Cowardice tore out the hold I once held so dear–
It was surgery, all along
Tumultuous waves crashing and drowning
a heart as pale and as ragged as mine

"Damaged people damage people,"
and that rule held true,
as we both sank on the same damned ship
sabotaged by you   and I,
            & the sins of both of us
the hopeful   and the unbeliever,
the fearful   and the faithless

Young Woman

"YOUNG WOMAN–
stay in your lane."
micro-aggressions hit like well-aimed knives
under unstable armor
catcalls turned into spiked cortisol,
hurrying home under city street lights
late nights at the metro leave me breathless
as train delays leave me waiting for 20, 30
minutes to get back to my safe house

I pray to gods I don't believe in,
I beg for one more safe night ride

YOUNG WOMAN–
stay in your lane...
under the cover of evening
it's unrealistic to fight misnomers
identity like egg yolk,
running over unexacting fingers
dripping through cracked shells

between fear-splattered nights I dodge
what it means to be on neither side

a non-binary warrior forging forward,
exploring the viability of life
on *no-man's land*
I root new meanings in fragile selfhood
I bury seeds in ravaged soil

on the battlefield between *manhood* and *womanhood*,
I wave my white flag.

How to Grieve Without Guilt

the bluebird outside my window instructs
those lost to grief to sing sweet songs
of *sorrow, honor*, and *eulogy*
though I know little of what night will bring
through a throat swollen with tears,
she instructs me to sing

write your eulogies *over*

and *over*

and *over*

cry and shake with the weight

mourn lost fathers, mothers,

                      & those that taught you to speak

be *loud* with your grief.

do not stop

         until

           you are ready to heal

scream   until the wails subside

dance relentlessly through sorrow

         run until your muscles grow steady,

move with the pain that teaches you

           and even then

carry the songs

of those that taught you   to sing

Our Song

Our love song is a waltz:
a partnered dance,

One plus one

equals...
equals...
equals...

skipping a beat,
just to return again

A Fair Exchange

that night, we were:
>dark dancers, teasing & moonlit

pupils ablaze with curiosity
>tethered bodies, caught in limbo

>betwixt ***Yes!*** and *Maybe*,

indulgent, bold & unresistant to
desire, giving away pleasure...

that morning, we were:
affectionate lovers, warmed by sun
sweat glistening on skin like morning dew
bruised peaches,
>with bite-marked skin.

Creator

I am a Creator
and you are a Creator, too
when our palms touch, I feel galaxies
emerge between our fingertips,
stars bursting from our knuckles,
our limbs are aching with the wonder of comet trails,
our lungs gasping with the weight of distant supernovas

I always saw the star in you;
                    I was lit alive by your divine enigmas
you were the sun, moon, and stars...
                    ...but you were not my whole galaxy.
I admire the comets that dance with me,
               when I am alone.
I enjoy the magnificent galaxy that I am,
               when I am alone.

Yellow

Osún loves yellow,
and I love Osún
we dance with the levity of honeybees,
warmed by sweet collective care,
dancing with the warm draw of honey
we are infinite in concept,
but endangered as individuals
we were not meant to exist alone

when you and I are intertwined, I think about the magic
of a hive, connected in common purpose
I wonder whether I am the *queen*, or another *worker bee*
I wonder if you know where you are traveling to
I wonder if we will both wander
when you wake, I catch your mind wandering
it seems that you are always just before waking

have you ever thought about the melodies that bees make?

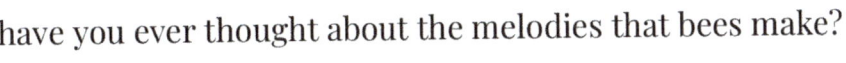

Moths Can Also Be Butterflies

your breath fogs on my glasses
like a fine mist of rain
and the moonlight reflects off
melanated skin like stars
shining on ivory

you look at me like I'm a shooting star,
exploding quickly across a muted sky
but never burning out,
never fading
moving quickly out of human perception

my desire for carefully chosen words
disappears when I look into your eyes
you pull truths out of me
that I wasn't even planning to give
but *hell*, I ain't even mad...
your captive attention is rich like honey
smoothing over my cracks like liquid gold

you are a *magician*—
you pull colors out of me that
I've never even seen before
and the intensity of being known
for all that I am,
and for all that I will *never* be
incites my galaxy back into motion

we are all planets in orbit around one another
and I feel you like the gentle tug of gravity,
pulling me back down to Earth
after a long journey through the stars

Reverie: Healed

Do you know the shape of your shadow?

I used to be afraid of the darkness,
Afraid that my melanin was not bright enough
to light up a room simply by existing in divinity;

For years, I hid inside my shadow.
Afraid to touch the world, and hesitant
for the world to touch me.

But all that I touch, reminds me that I have changed
                        Now I dance with sunlight, dabbling in rays of warmth

like I was **born here**,
because it is my divine birthright
to shine without shame,
to touch the world without apology.
All of me that I touch,
is all of me that is healed.

Freedom Song

I am free
free as the wind that wraps around my feet
as free as the grass beneath my toes
free like humanity never tried
to put a yoke on me;
never tried to make a slave outta me
never tried to build a new empire outta me.

I am free
Because I told myself I would be
I am free because I am an agent
of sweet Liberty, a concept as divine as it is
often just outta reach,
because my skin, golden as I am,
was never made to equate to the freedom of a dollar bill,
or the freedom of a living wage plus benefits,
or the freedom of an all-access pass to every room I ever wished to enter

My freedom waits for me,
Because my freedom knows I am on the way.

Born to Fly

Damn, loved one, were you born this fly?

Fly-ass fro,

Curled up wash-and-go

And bold-bright melanin that lights up the room

Enough swag to spread those wings and

Be a bird of a feather,

    Iridescent in any & every weather

Fly enough to hang with the sisters

With the foresight to set trends in vogue

Because baby, *we flock together*!

We stand tall with our transgender sisters, non-binary friends,

    and trans-masculine shapeshifters,

growing strong community   with the knowledge that

    gender was *never* meant to be a gatekeeper,

but it keeps us safe in numbers outside the gate!

And those metal bars never stopped our rise:

    We stand *strong* in the face of terror.

    We *stand up,* we protect one another.

    We protect our queer & trans sisters.

    We stand tall for our gender-bending brothers.

All while taking care for those

                    who can't care for themselves.

All while holding the very world on our benevolent backs.

Never pinned down by the accusations of the world,

And *always* ready to shake the weight—

Because we are more than your caretakers.

Refusing to be painted into the role of *mammy*—

We color boldly outside the lines.

We walk in defiance of your rule book,

And we see right through the lies:

Black people were born to fly.

black and blue

Afterword

This book would not have been possible without community. When I first began my journey with *Black and Blue*, I found power and inspiration through the works of Nikky Finney, Kamau Brathwaite, Saidiya Hartman, and Jericho Brown. As I moved forward with editing, curating, and publishing, I was held tight with the courage of Audre Lorde, the inspirations of Maya Angelou, the cutting words of James Baldwin, and the spirited gall of Toni Morrison. At each stage, I bit back waves of fear and swallowed the words bubbling up in my throat at each turn:

What if I'm not good enough?
What if my words don't matter?

This chapbook contains 9 years of poetry, written at bus stops and in between long shifts. This book captures the raw truth of the experience that I lived and breathed, while exploring the complicated trip lines of class, gender, and racial bias.

Black and Blue is a portal between the historical realities of Western culture and the cutting words of those who have finally had enough. My poetry documents a personal journey that dances alongside historical lines, blending my individual experience with ancestral memory and intergenerational knowledge. While the poetry within this book is deeply rooted in cultural observations and historical truths, each poem is deeply personal to my own experience as a Black, queer, non-binary person, sometimes masc and sometimes femme and sometimes a vehement *neither–* I am often mistaken for what I am not. As a historian and community storyteller, I took care in blending my own stories with the experiences of the ancestors, storytellers, historians, and record-keepers that came before me. We do not all have the capacity to be categorized. We do not all care to be named. Our words will dare to live after us.

For every writer still wondering whether their story is good enough to share:

Your work is good enough.
Your words do indeed matter.
You have the power to change the world.

And in the case that these words are not enough to lift you into action, to encourage you to *uncut your tongue* and release your truth, I offer the apt words of Toni Cade Bambara, which prompted me through many aching moments of fear and worry and doubt and disbelief:

Do not leave the arena to the fools.

Credits

My journey with *Black and Blue* was directly inspired by my studies of African diasporic history and literature. As I journeyed along the troubled path of history, those studies were inevitably impacted by the literary works of powerful authors within the arena of African–American literature, critical theory, and academic thought.

In the spirit of collaboration, it only feels appropriate to name the books that most deeply rooted and nourished my writing for *Black and Blue:*

Claudia Rankine, *Citizen*
Jericho Brown, *The Tradition*
Nikky Finney, *Head off and Split*
Kamau Brathwaite, *Middle Passages*
Saidiya Hartman, *Scenes of Subjection*
Audre Lorde, *Zami: A New Spelling of My Name*

It has been an honor to write and dream alongside so many powerful minds. Thank you for inspiring through apt historical, social, and interpersonal commentary.

Thank you to the powerful writers and poets who came before me, and to the many others who inspired me to act: your support raises me on wings of silk.

BLUEBOY PUBLISHING HOUSE

MISSION STATEMENT

EMPOWER BLACK CREATIVES

Blueboy Publishing House is a Black-owned publishing company dedicated to helping underrepresented authors thrive in the world of publishing. As an independent publishing house, we uplift Black creative thinkers by investing in compelling stories and providing services to expanding authors.

INSPIRE CREATIVE CULTURE

Blueboy Publishing House is dedicated to uplifting rising writers with powerful stories, bringing attention to underrepresented cultures and identities. As a growing team of directors, creators, and artists: we believe in uplifting strong community values as we intentionally shift our culture to embody the voices of change-makers, healers, and visionary thinkers.

PROMOTE NEW IDEAS

As we expand creatively into this new era, we face a revolutionary new wave of artists and culture-makers. At Blueboy Publishing House, we are invested in promoting fresh new ideas that represent the power we have to change the world.

Publisher Information

Blueboy Publishing House, Inc.

Mailing Address – California:
954 E. Badillo Street
Unit #2244
Covina, California 91724

Please do not send unsolicited mail.

Web: www.blueboypublishinghouse.com
Email: info@blueboypublishinghouse.com
Social: @blueboypublishinghouse

Please direct all professional inquiries to our company email.

About the Author

Dorian Blue (they/them) is a multidisciplinary creator, visionary storyteller, dream-weaver, and poet from Washington, DC.

Dorian Blue believes in storytelling as a powerful vehicle for liberation & catharsis.

Existing at the crux of Black/autistic/queer/femme/non-binary provides a colorful (yet narrow) tightrope of experience. The clever learn to walk it, or fall trying.

Be mindful of your stories: we choose new histories every day.

www.blueboypublishinghouse.com

Upcoming Releases

Visit our website for more information on upcoming releases, calls for entries, book events, and updates to our catalogue.

Black and Blue: A Liberation Anthology

Cradled gently in a dialect of imagination and honesty, Dorian Blue conjures an alluring collection of multidimensional storytelling that dives deep into the social, cultural, and historical experiences of the queer Black body.

Mythos

Mythos is a fresh literary collection of mythologies, passages, and short stories that unpack the connection between *power* and *tradition*.

Details to be announced.

The Dark Side of the Moon

In the year 3020, amidst a world decimated by the effects of climate change, a specialized class of genetically modified *kraken* survive by attaching to unmodified humans, using electrochemical attraction to lure willing lovers to an early death.

City of Secrets

Dare to slip into a reality different than your own: into a hidden world that offers a mysterious new landscape, fascinating questions, and a different point of view.

Details to be announced.

Find out more about upcoming releases at www.blueboypublishinghouse.com

www.ingramcontent.com/pod-product-compliance
Lightning Source LLC
Chambersburg PA
CBHW041540120626
46551CB00019B/2778